# Flavours
## of the
# Spice Coast

# Flavours
## of the
# Spice Coast

## Mrs K M Mathew

PENGUIN BOOKS

PENGUIN BOOKS
Published by the Penguin Group
Penguin Books India Pvt. Ltd, 11 Community Centre, Panchsheel Park,
New Delhi 110 017, India
Penguin Group (USA) Inc., 375 Hudson Street, New York, New York 10014, USA
Penguin Group (Canada), 90 Eglinton Avenue East, Suite 700, Toronto, Ontario, M4P
2Y3, Canada (a division of Pearson Penguin Canada Inc.)
Penguin Books Ltd, 80 Strand, London WC2R 0RL, England
Penguin Ireland, 25 St Stephen's Green, Dublin 2, Ireland (a division of Penguin Books Ltd)
Penguin Group (Australia), 250 Camberwell Road, Camberwell, Victoria 3124, Australia
(a division of Pearson Australia Group Pty Ltd)
Penguin Group (NZ), 67 Apollo Drive, Rosedale, Auckland 0632, New Zealand
(a division of Pearson New Zealand Ltd)
Penguin Group (South Africa) (Pty) Ltd, 24 Sturdee Avenue, Rosebank, Johannesburg
2196, South Africa

Penguin Books Ltd, Registered Offices: 80 Strand, London WC2R 0RL, England

First published in Viking by Penguin Books India 2002
Published in Penguin Books 2002

Copyright © Mrs K.M. Mathew 2002

15  14  13  12  11  10  9

ISBN  9780143029007

Typeset in S.R. Enterprises, New Delhi
Printed at Sanat Printers, Kundli, Haryana

ALWAYS LEARNING          **PEARSON**

# Contents

# Foreword

I am delighted to have the honour of writing this foreword to a cookbook by my dear friend Mrs K.M. Mathew.

Annamma, as Mrs Mathew is popularly known, is a connoisseur of art—be it music, dancing, flower arrangement or food festivals. All those who have enjoyed her hospitality know the culinary excellence she has achieved.

With her moorings in the ethos of Kerala cuisine, Annamma is an ideal hostess who knows the art of reaching out, beyond the table.

I am sure this beautifully crafted book will enrich the young and old whose passion is to entertain with culinary delights.

Best wishes to Annamma.

Thangam Philip.
T.E Philip's

Kaudiar Palace
15 October, 2001

Mrs K.M. Mathew, famous wife of a famous husband, is a popular figure not only in her home state, Kerala, but at the national level as well. While her name lends itself to many good causes, Mrs Mathew is perhaps best known for her expertise in culinary art, with her recipe books being accorded an impressive welcome in the homes of many in India and overseas. Over the years she has almost become a household name in this field, with many of her recipes proving to be innovative and interesting. Her range is vast and geared to suit every budget, from the luxurious to the spartan. While many honours have come her way, perhaps the greatest recognition is the unwavering demand for and acceptance of her books. Her success lies in the fact that she has not only introduced very many to the delights of the kitchen, but also delights, mother-like, in cooking up fabulous meals for all those who cross her path.

I am sure that this beautifully brought out book, a gift of love from the family that holds her so dear, will be very well received. Being a pure vegetarian though, I cannot help hoping that some day she will write a totally vegetarian companion to this edition.

I wish her many more fruitful years of active and satisfying life, with the grace of God.

Aswathi Thirunal
PRINCESS OF TRAVANCORE

# Acknowledgements

My interest in food came very early in life. Dr George Philip, my father, was a very special person and a food lover who spent much of his free time in our kitchen and always filled it with amazingly appetizing smells. He inspired in me an abiding interest in the art of cooking and taught me the magic of flavours.

Cooking would have remained a passion only at home if my father-in-law K.C. Mammen Mappillai had not encouraged me to write a column of my recipes in *Malayala Manorama*, his newspaper, in 1953. He was no doubt courageous! As has been my husband, K.M. Mathew, who has sampled all my culinary creations with great fortitude. He has been my wildest admirer and sweetest critic, though he may deadpan that he is my gastronomic guinea pig. My immediate family—my children, their spouses and my grandchildren—have also always made it a point to laud my efforts.

Several others have contributed to the making of this book. I would like to express my love and gratitude in particular to:

Indu B. Nair, my dear friend and colleague, who has diligently drafted and compiled my recipes for over two decades.

P. N. Vasu and Sylvester D'Souza, the finest chefs in the world, who have for decades assisted me in my experiments with new recipes. Kunjumon Chacko, for his aesthetic eye that immensely enhanced the visual appeal of the dishes.

All the staff at *Vanitha*; especially Manarcad Mathew, who has always been a generator of excellent ideas.

The talented Suchi Ebrahim, who conceptualized the visual appeal of my book and enriched it with her design. The wonderful wordsmith, Mini Krishnan, who translated the recipes into English, and edited the book.

K. Mohan Rangan, the wizard with the camera, who has made the dishes look irresistibly delicious; Salim Pushpanath for his photograph of the 'sadya'.

*Malayala Manorama* Delhi Resident Editor, Sachidananda Murthy, who introduced me to Penguin India, and V.S. Jayachandran, chief copy editor of *The Week,* who helped craft the written word.

I thank all of them for their enthusiasm and energy, and wish them pure joy in life.

Happy cooking.

Annamma Mathew

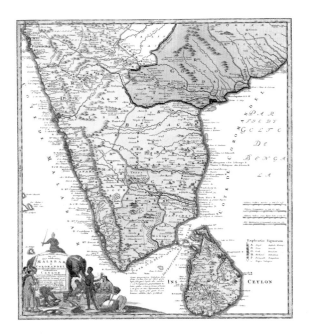

## The setting...

Middleman to the ancient world, laced by forty-one rivers and a thousand canals, Kerala lies like a jewel fixed to the southwestern coast of India, a 580 kilometre-long stretch. The demand for pepper (often called black gold) and other spices drew traders to this land more than two thousand years ago. Food and flavour, the great levellers, brought international influences to Kerala in the first millennium in the form of peaceful traders from Arabia, Egypt, Greece, Phoenecia, China and the Roman empire.

Historical evidence shows that Apostle St. Thomas (the doubting Thomas) converted Hindus in AD 52 at Muziris (present-day Kodungallur, Kerala). Historians agree that Christians have been here for fifteen centuries. Muslims have evidence of a mosque in Kerala even before the death of Prophet Mohammed. Jews have lived here since the first century AD. The descendants of all these denominations have lived side by side with Kerala's Hindu majority for generations, creating a cosmopolitan state.

Goods from South India had reached the Middle East as early as the third millennium BC when, stimulated by the Roman demand for exotic goods and the discovery of the monsoon winds by Greek sailors (about AD 45), ships serving Rome began to sail from the Horn of Africa to Kerala in five weeks' time. This shifted the focus of the spice trade from North Indian ports and land routes to Muziris, which the Roman historian Pliny called 'the first commercial centre of India'.

Indian and Malay merchants pushed eastwards, collecting silk and cinnamon from China and precious stones and tortoise shells from Indonesia, to be loaded onto Greek and Persian ships at Muziris, which was positioned midway along the spice route between the Roman Empire and China.

More than a thousand years later, the lure of spices and luxury goods attracted a new crowd of merchant adventurers to South India: the Portuguese, the Dutch, the French, and finally the English. They too left behind their cultures, languages and ideas.

It was trade and food that launched Kerala in the hospitality business and today, the state is one of the world's favourite destinations.

# The writer...

About fifty years ago, a Malayalam newspaper sandwiched a recipe for mutton between reports on prime ministers Nehru and Churchill. The six-inch recipe column which appeared in a June 1953 edition of *Malayala Manorama*, had only a mustard-sized byline: Mrs Annamma Mathew. But it marked the advent of a remarkable epicurean who was to inspire millions of Malayali women to cook well and cook sensibly–for the writer was actually Mrs K.M. Mathew, who was almost singlehandedly responsible for taking the flavours of Kerala's dim, smoke-filled kitchens to glamorous dining rooms across the world.

It was almost the first time that a recipe was appearing in print in Kerala, and the dish she prescribed in meticulous detail had the aroma of novelty. After this she went on to offer recipes, ethnic and exotic, in a regular media column, 'Pachaka Vidhi', which, like well-made wine, only improved with age. Over the years she compiled her writings into more than twenty cookbooks, all best-sellers both in and outside her home state.

Her larder of ideas was always brimming over, and her recipes for the myriad new dishes she invented sprung from her conviction that nutritious food need not necessarily be rich and expensive. For example, she experimented with an ordinary and abundantly available root like the humble tapioca and gave it a place of honour on the dinner table.

Cooking was a dull chore in sooty Kerala kitchens before Mrs Mathew's delicious experimentations; her writings elevated cooking into an exciting experience for a large number of women. The new skills and knowledge worked wonders for their confidence and self-esteem, and if something else was cooking, it was women's liberation.

Mrs Mathew further shaped women's sensibilities as the founder editor of *Vanitha*, the first Malayalam publication exclusively devoted to women. It virtually redefined the identity of Malayali women, encouraging them to be fearless and independent and at the same time to be caring and nurturing and, most importantly, vocal about their feelings. Founded in 1975, the magazine showcased women's aspirations and achievements and its popularity has ever been on the rise; it is the best-selling women's magazine in India and boasts a fortnightly circulation of 3,69,220 copies. Today *Vanitha* has a Hindi edition too. In this sense, Mrs Mathew was a pioneering feminist publisher.

Her work in journalism fetched Mrs Mathew a number of awards, including the Vigjanadeepam Puraskar (1994) instituted by the Ponnara Sreedhar Foundation and the Nirmithi Kendra Award (1996) by a state-run organization that initiated a housing revolution in Kerala. In 1992 she was conferred the Rachel Thomas Award for her outstanding contribution to social and cultural causes.

When not wading through journalistic copy or stir-frying something at the numerous cooking classes she organized out of sheer love for the art, Mrs Mathew guided the Kasturba Social Welfare Centre in Kottayam, which conducts vocational courses, art classes and study tours. Her relaxations were playing the violin and guitar and listening to Carnatic music.

# Meat

1  Mutton Chops

2  Mutton Kurma

3  Mutton Red Curry

4  Meat Pattichu Varathathu

5  Meat Oolarthiyathu

6  Meat Stew

7  Spicy Curried Dumplings

8  Easter Chicken Roast

9  Chicken Piralen

10  Trivandrum Chicken

11  Ellu Chicken

12  Duck Curry

13  Duck Roast

# Mutton Chops

*You will need :*

1  500 gms tender mutton, on the rib
2  salt to taste
3  $1/2$ cup water
4  $1/4$ cup refined vegetable oil
5  $3/4$ cup onion, finely chopped
6  $1/2$ tsp garlic paste
7  $1/2$ tsp ginger paste
8  $3/4$ tsp chilli powder
9  $1/2$ tsp pepper powder
10  $1/4$ tsp turmeric powder
11  1 dsp lime juice
12  $1/2$ tsp cumin seeds
13  2 cloves
14  2" cinnamon
15  1 cardamom pod

*To serve 5*

*Method :*

1  Wash and clean the mutton. Cook on low fire with salt and $1/2$ cup water. Drain the mutton and reserve a cup of stock.

2  Heat oil in a skillet, add chopped onion and fry till well browned.

3  Add garlic and ginger paste and fry to a golden colour.

4  Mix ingredients 8 to 10 with a little water to make a paste and add to the fried ingredients. Fry well.

5  Add the meat and brown well.

6  Pour in the stock and lime juice, reduce heat and simmer for 10 minutes.

7  Powder items 12 to 15 and add the powdered ingredients to the mutton.

8  When the gravy thickens remove from heat. Serve hot.

## Mutton Kurma

### You will need :

1   ³/₄ kg mutton
2   1 cup hot water
3   2" cinnamon
4   1 tsp cloves
5   1 tsp cardamom pods
6   salt to taste
7   ¹/₂ cup refined vegetable oil
8   ¹/₂ kg onions, sliced
9   1 cup ghee
10  2 dsp garlic paste
11  2 dsp ginger paste
12  1 tsp coriander powder
13  ¹/₂ tsp turmeric powder
14  1 tsp chilli powder
15  2 tsp aniseed
16  ¹/₄ kg tomatoes, chopped
17  1 cup curd
18  a handful of coriander leaves
19  4 green chillies, slit
20  ¹/₄ cup cashewnuts
21  ¹/₂ cup coconut, grated
22  lime juice to taste

*To serve 5*

### Method :

1   Cut the mutton into medium-size pieces. Trim aw
    the excess fat and wash well.
2   Cook the mutton with 1 cup hot water a
    ingredients 3 to 6. Cover with a deep lid contain
    water on top. Reduce heat and cook at a ger
    simmer till the mutton is tender and the stock
    reduced to one cup. Remove from heat and ke
    aside.
3   Heat oil in a pan and fry the sliced onions, stirr
    frequently. Wait till they turn a golden brov
    Remove from heat and keep aside.
4   Heat the ghee in another pan. Fry the garlic a
    the ginger paste one after the other.
5   Grind ingredients 12 to 15 to a paste. Add this
    the fried garlic ginger paste. Fry well.
6   Add the chopped tomatoes. Fry well until the
    separates. Add curd, coriander leaves, gre
    chillies, fried onion and cooked meat with the spic
    and the stock. Mix well. Cover with a lid.
7   Reduce heat and simmer for about 10 minutes
    the meat pieces are blended well with the grav
8   Grind the cashewnuts and the grated coconut i
    a fine paste. Blend this paste into the curry a
    mix well. Add lime juice and salt to taste. Remo
    from fire. Serve hot.

# Mutton Red Curry

*You will need :*

| | |
|---|---|
| 1 | 1 kg mutton |
| 2 | 2 dsp chilli powder |
| 3 | 1 tsp coriander powder |
| 4 | 1 tsp mustard seeds |
| 5 | 1/4 tsp fenugreek seeds |
| 6 | 1/2 tsp cumin seeds |
| 7 | 1 tsp ginger, sliced |
| 8 | 1 tsp garlic cloves |
| 9 | 1 1/2 dsp vinegar |
| 10 | 1/2 cup refined vegetable oil |
| 11 | 2 cups onion, finely sliced |
| 12 | 250 gms ripe tomatoes, finely chopped |
| 13 | salt to taste |
| 14 | 3 cups hot water |

*To serve 10*

*Method :*

1  Wash and clean the mutton. Cut into medium-size pieces.
2  Grind items 2 to 8 with vinegar into a paste.
3  Heat oil, sauté sliced onions and add chopped tomatoes. Fry well and add the ground paste.
4  Fry on low flame till the oil rises to the surface. Add the meat pieces and salt. Mix well.
5  Add 3 cups hot water to cook the meat.
6  Cover the vessel with a deep lid containing boiling water. This will help the meat to cook well.
7  Keep on low heat and simmer until the gravy starts thickening.
8  Once the meat is cooked, remove from fire and serve warm.

## Meat Pattichu Varathathu

*You will need :*

1. 500 gms of any red meat
2. 1 dsp chilli powder
3. 1 dsp coriander powder
4. 1/4 tsp turmeric powder
5. 1/4 tsp pepper powder
6. 6 garlic cloves, sliced
7. 1/2 tsp aniseed
8. 2 cloves
9. 1" cinnamon
10. 1 dsp vinegar
11. 1/2 tsp ginger, chopped
12. salt to taste
13. 2 cups hot water
14. 2 small potatoes, diced
15. 1 tsp garlic cloves

*For the seasoning :*

1. 2 dsp coconut oil or any cooking oil
2. 1/4 tsp mustard seeds
3. 2 dsp button onions, sliced

*To serve 5*

*Method :*

1. Wash and clean the meat. Cut meat into large cubes.
2. Grind into a paste ingredients 2 to 9. Marinate the meat with the ground paste, vinegar, chopped ginger and salt for an hour.
3. Cook the meat in 2 cups hot water. Cover the pan with a deep lid containing water. This water will help cook the meat as well as ensure that it does not get charred.
4. When the meat is tender, add the potatoes and garlic.
5. When the potato is well cooked and the gravy has thickened, remove from fire.
6. In another pan, heat coconut oil and add mustard seeds.
7. When it splutters, add the button onions.
8. When the button onions are browned, add the meat mixture.
9. Fry till dry, taking care not to let the potato pieces crumble.
10. When the masala leaves the sides of the pan, remove from heat and serve hot.

*Note :*
If you are not a habitual user of coconut oil, substitute with any oil.

# Meat Oolarthiyathu

*You will need :*

1   1 kg mutton or chicken
2   ³/₄ dsp chilli powder
3   1 dsp coriander powder
4   ¹/₂ tsp turmeric powder
5   ¹/₂ tsp peppercorns
6   ¹/₂ tsp cumin seeds
7   1 tsp aniseed
8   2" cinnamon
9   3 cloves
10  2 cardamom pods
11  ¹/₂ cup button onions, sliced
12  8 garlic cloves
13  2 tsp ginger, sliced long
14  a few curry leaves
15  ¹/₂ cup coconut, sliced thin and small,
      smeared with salt and turmeric and fried
16  1 dsp vinegar
17  salt to taste
18  1 cup hot water

*For the seasoning :*

1   ¹/₄ cup refined vegetable oil
2   1 tsp mustard seeds
3   2 dsp onion, finely chopped

*Method :*

1   Wash and clean the meat. Cut into
    medium-size pieces.
2   Grind into a paste ingredients 2 to 10.
3   Cook the meat, adding the ground
    paste and ingredients 11 to 18. After
    the meat is tender and coated with a
    little gravy, remove from fire.
4   Heat oil, splutter mustard seeds, and
    fry the onion. Stir in the meat and fry
    well until dry.

*To serve 10*

# Meat Stew

## You will need :

1. 1 kg mutton or chicken
2. 3 potatoes
3. ¼ cup refined vegetable oil
4. 1 cup onion, sliced
5. 1 dsp garlic, sliced
6. 1 dsp ginger, sliced
7. 6 green chillies, slit
8. 2" cinnamon
9. 6 cloves
10. 4 cardamom pods
11. 1 dsp peppercorns
12. a few curry leaves
13. 2 dsp vinegar
14. salt to taste
15. 2 cups thin coconut milk
16. ¾ cup thick coconut milk

*To serve 10*

## Method :

1. Wash and clean the meat. Trim the fat. Cut into pieces.
2. Peel and cut the potatoes into wedges.
3. Heat the oil in a pan, add ingredients 4 to 12 and gently fry until soft and golden.
4. Add the meat and fry gently.
5. Add vinegar, salt and the thin coconut milk.
6. When the meat is half cooked, add the potato wedges.
7. Cover the pan with a well-fitting lid and cook until the meat is tender.
8. When the gravy has reduced in quantity, add ¾ cup thick coconut milk and bring to boil. Remove from fire and serve hot.

## You will need :

### For the dumplings :

1   ¹/₂ kg minced meat
2   1 tsp chilli powder
3   2 dsp coriander powder
4   ¹/₂ tsp turmeric powder
5   ¹/₄ tsp pepper powder
6   ¹/₄ tsp cumin seeds
7   2" cinnamon
8   2 cardamom pods
9   ¹/₂ tsp aniseed
10  2 dsp button onions,
     finely chopped
11  ¹/₂ dsp green chillies, chopped
12  ¹/₂ dsp ginger, chopped
13  ¹/₂ dsp garlic, chopped
14  salt to taste

### For the gravy :

1   ¹/₄ cup refined vegetable oil
2   ¹/₄ cup onion, sliced
3   ¹/₄ tsp garlic, sliced
4   1 tsp ginger, julliened
5   4 green chillies, slit
6   2 cups thin coconut milk
7   1 dsp vinegar
8   salt to taste
9   a few curry leaves
10  ¹/₂ cup thick coconut milk

# Spicy Curried Dumplings

## Method :

1   Wash and clean the minced meat.
2   Grind items 2 to 9 to a fine paste for the masala.
3   Mix together the minced meat, the finely chopped button onions, green chillies, ginger and garlic with 2 tsp of the ground masala and salt and shape into balls.
4   Heat oil and sauté the sliced onion, garlic, ginger and green chillies.
5   Add the remaining ground masala and fry well until the oil separates.
6   Add the thin coconut milk, vinegar, salt and curry leaves.
7   When the gravy begins to bubble, gently drop in the prepared meat balls.
8   Continue cooking until the meat is tender and the gravy has reduced in quantity.
9   Add the thick coconut milk, bring the curry to boil and remove from the fire. Serve hot.

*To serve 5*

# Easter Chicken Roast

## Method :

1 Wash and dry chicken inside and out. Grind items 2 to 5 to a fine paste. Add salt and vinegar.

2 Rub well over the chicken. Marinate in a covered bowl for three hours.

3 Heat oil in a deep pan and brown the chicken over low heat, turning it over occasionally to ensure even cooking.

4 Pour hot water over the meat and cook till tender.

5 When tender, remove the meat from its gravy and set aside.

6 Cook the gravy until it thickens and the oil separates.

7 Drain the excess oil, return the chicken to the pan and cook over low heat until it is well coated with the gravy.

*To serve 6*

## You will need :

1 1 whole chicken (remove liver and kidney)

2 $1/2$ tsp turmeric powder

3 1 tsp chilli powder

4 2" cinnamon

5 6 cloves

6 salt to taste

7 1 dsp vinegar

8 2 dsp refined oil

9 1 $1/4$ cup hot water

## Chicken Piralen

**You will need :**

1   1 kg chicken
2   1½ dsp coriander powder
3   1 dsp chilli powder
4   ½ tsp turmeric powder
5   ½ tsp pepper powder
6   ½ tsp cumin seeds
7   1" cinnamon
8   8 cloves
9   4 cardamom pods
10  1 tsp aniseed
11  ¼ cup button onions, sliced
12  1 dsp garlic, chopped
13  ½ dsp ginger, finely chopped
14  salt to taste
15  1 dsp vinegar
16  a few curry leaves
17  ½ cup hot water
18  ¼ cup refined vegetable oil

**Method :**

1   Wash and clean the chicken. Cut into pieces of desired size.
2   Grind into a paste ingredients 2 to 10.
3   Blend the masala into the chicken pieces. Add ingredients 11 to 16.
4   Add hot water to cook the chicken. Turn heat low, cover and cook until chicken is tender.
5   When it is cooked and the gravy has thickened, remove from fire. Separate the chicken pieces from the gravy.
6   Heat oil.
7   Add the chicken pieces and fry until brown.
8   Pour the gravy over and fry until the chicken pieces are coated with it.
9   Serve hot.

*To serve 10*

# Trivandrum Chicken

## You will need :

1   1 kg chicken
2   3 dsp chilli powder
3   1" ginger, chopped
4   10 garlic cloves
5   10 button onions
6   1 dsp aniseed
7   2 dsp lime juice
8   1/4 tsp red food colouring
9   4 dsp rice flour
10  1/4 kg coconut oil

*To serve 10*

## Method :

1   Wash and clean the chicken. Cut into large pieces and make gashes in it.
2   Grind into a paste ingredients 2 to 6.
3   Add the lime juice and colouring to the ground paste and rub the chicken pieces with it.
4   Keep in a cool place for four hours.
5   Sprinkle the rice flour over and fry the chicken pieces in hot coconut oil.
6   The residue of the fried flour should be drained and sprinkled on the chicken pieces. Serve hot.

*Note :*
Coconut oil tastes better, but any other cooking oil can also be used.

# Ellu Chicken

### You will need :

1. 1 kg chicken
2. 2 tsp garlic, chopped
3. 2 tsp ginger, chopped
4. 6 green chillies
5. 1 tsp peppercorns
6. 1 tsp turmeric powder
7. 2 dsp lime juice
8. salt to taste
9. 2 cups hot water
10. 2 eggs, beaten
11. 1 cup bread crumbs
12. 3 dsp white & black mixed sesame seeds
13. oil to fry

### For the gravy :

1. 1 tsp butter
2. 1 tsp rice flour

### Method :

1. Wash and clean the chicken. Cut into ten pieces.
2. Grind into a paste ingredients 2 to 6. Add lime juice and mix the chicken pieces with the ground paste.
3. Add salt to taste and cook the chicken in hot water. When the chicken is cooked, there should be $1/2$ cup stock left for the gravy.
4. Separate the chicken pieces from the gravy.
5. Dip the cooked pieces of chicken in beaten egg.
6. Coat well by rolling in bread crumbs mixed with sesame seeds.
7. Heat oil in a shallow pan, deep fry the chicken and serve hot with a bowl of gravy.

### To make the gravy :

1. Melt the butter. Add the flour and brown. Add the stock and stir to make a gravy.

### Note :

Try using the same recipe for mutton chops.

*To serve 10 persons*

## Duck Curry

### You will need :

1. 1 kg duck
2. 2 dsp coriander powder
3. 2 tsp chilli powder
4. 1/4 tsp turmeric powder
5. 2" cinnamon
6. 6 cloves
7. 4 cardamom pods
8. 1 tsp aniseed
9. 4 potatoes
10. 1/4 cup refined vegetable oil
11. 1/2 cup onion, sliced long and thin
12. 2 tsp ginger, sliced long and thin
13. 8 garlic cloves
14. 6 green chillies, slit
15. 2 dsp vinegar
16. salt to taste
17. 3 cups thin coconut milk
18. 1 cup thick coconut milk

### For the seasoning :

1. 1 dsp refined vegetable oil
2. 1 tsp ghee
3. 1 tsp mustard seeds
4. 2 dsp button onions, sliced
5. a few curry leaves

### Method :

1. Wash and clean the duck.
2. Cut the duck into 8 to 10 pieces.
3. Grind into a paste ingredients 2 to 8.
4. Peel and quarter the potatoes.
5. Heat the oil, add the sliced onion, ginger, garlic and green chillies and fry well to a golden brown.
6. Add the ground paste and sauté.
7. Add meat, vinegar and salt.
8. Stir for 5 minutes to blend all the ingredients.
9. Stir in the thin coconut milk, cover the pan with a well-fitting lid and cook the duck.
10. When the duck is done, add the quartered potatoes.
11. After the duck and potatoes are cooked, add the thick coconut milk and remove from fire.
12. Heat the oil and ghee.
13. Splutter the mustard seeds and gently fry the sliced button onions and curry leaves.
14. Add this seasoning to the curry.
15. Serve hot.

*To serve 10*

## Duck Roast

*You will need :*

1  1 kg duck
2  2 dsp coriander powder
3  2 tsp chilli powder
4  $1/2$ tsp turmeric powder
5  1 tsp peppercorns
6  1 tsp aniseed
7  2" cinnamon
8  9 cloves
9  2 cardamom pods
10  8 garlic cloves
11  1" ginger
12  1 dsp vinegar
13  salt to taste
14  2 cups hot water
15  3 potatoes, parboiled and quartered lengthwise
16  2 dsp ghee
17  $1/4$ cup refined vegetable oil
18  $1/2$ cup onion, sliced, soaked in salt water and squeezed dry
19  1 cup thick coconut milk

*To serve 6*

*Method :*

1  Wash and clean the duck. Cut into large pieces.
2  Grind into a paste ingredients 2 to 11.
3  Add vinegar and salt. Apply this paste on the duck pieces.
4  Add 2 cups hot water and cook the duck, covering the pan with a tight-fitting lid.
5  When the duck is cooked, separate the pieces from the gravy.
6  Fry the potatoes in ghee and oil. Drain and keep aside.
7  In the same pan, fry onion and keep aside.
8  Fry the cooked pieces of duck in the remaining oil, adding more oil if necessary. Drain and keep aside.
9  Drain the oil from the pan.
10  Pour the masala gravy into the same pan and add the fried onion.
11  When this boils, add the fried pieces of duck and cook until all the gravy has been absorbed.
12  Add the coconut milk.
13  Remove from fire and serve the roast with the potatoes around it.

# Egg

1     Egg Curry

2     Egg Roast

## You will need :

1   6 eggs
2   1 dsp coriander powder
3   1 tsp chilli powder
4   1/4 tsp turmeric powder
5   1/4 tsp pepper powder
6   1" cinnamon
7   3 cloves
8   2 cardamom pods
9   2 dsp oil
10  1/4 cup onion, finely sliced
11  3 green chillies, half slit
12  1 tsp ginger, sliced
13  9 garlic cloves
14  1 dsp vinegar
15  1 1/2 cups thin coconut milk
16  salt to taste
17  2 potatoes, medium sized
18  1/2 cup thick coconut milk

## For the seasoning :

1   1/2 dsp oil
2   1/2 tsp ghee
3   1/2 tsp mustard seeds
4   1 dsp onion, sliced
5   a few curry leaves

# Egg Curry

## Method :

1   Hard boil and shell the eggs and set aside.
2   Grind ingredients 2 to 8 to a fine paste.
3   Heat oil and fry the onion, green chillies, ginger and garlic. Add the masala paste and fry well.
4   Dilute the vinegar with thin coconut milk and add salt.
5   Stir into the masala and bring to boil.
6   Cut the potatoes into quarters, add to the gravy, and cook until done.
7   Add the thick coconut milk and bring to boil once more. Halve the boiled eggs and add to the gravy. Remove from fire.
8   Heat oil and ghee. Splutter mustard seeds, add onion and curry leaves and fry lightly. Pour over curry. Serve hot.

To serve 6

# Egg Roast

*You will need :*

1   3 eggs
2   1$\frac{1}{2}$ tsp chilli powder
3   1$\frac{1}{2}$ tsp coriander powder
4   1 tsp pepper powder
5   $\frac{1}{2}$ tsp aniseed
6   1" cinnamon
7   2 cloves
8   1 cardamom pod
9   3 dsp refined vegetable oil
10  1 cup onion, sliced
11  $\frac{1}{4}$ cup tomato, chopped
12  salt to taste
13  $\frac{1}{4}$ cup water

*To serve 3*

*Method :*

1   Hard boil and shell the eggs. Keep aside.
2   Grind to a paste the chilli powder, coriander powder, pepper powder, aniseed and all the spices.
3   Heat the oil and fry onion till transparent. Add the ground paste and on low heat fry until oil oozes out. Stir in the tomatoes and continue frying on low heat. After the tomatoes are blended well, add salt and $\frac{1}{2}$ cup water. Cover and simmer till the gravy is thick. Halve the eggs and arrange on a serving dish. Pour the gravy over. Serve hot.

# Fish

1. Meen Peera Pattichathu (Fish with Grated Coconut)
2. Fish Masala
3. Meen Pollichathu (Fish Roasted in a Plantain Leaf)
4. Fish with Mango
5. Fish Molee
6. Fried Fish
7. Meen Vevichathu (Red Fish Curry)
8. Mathi Vattichathu (Sardines Cooked Dry)
9. Masala Pomfret
10. Prawn Oolarthiyathu
11. Prawn Pappas

## Meen Peera Pattichathu
### (Fish with Grated Coconut)

*You will need :*

1   ¹/₂ kg fish fillets or any small fish
2   2 cups coconut, grated
3   10 button onions
4   ¹/₂" ginger
5   4-5 green chillies, sliced
6   6 garlic cloves
7   ¹/₂ tsp turmeric powder
8   a few curry leaves
9   salt to taste
10  3 pieces cocum (fish tamarind), soaked in water and shredded
11  1 cup water
12  2 dsp oil, preferably coconut oil

*Method :*

1   Clean fish well in salted water.
2   Crush coconut, onions, ginger, chillies and garlic under a grinding stone. Add the turmeric powder.
3   Mix in the raw fish with the crushed ingredients, curry leaves and salt to taste.
4   Put the mixture in a pan or an earthenware vessel, add the cocum and one cup water to cock the fish.
5   Bring to boil, lower the heat and allow the mixture to dry out, taking care to see that the curry does not stick to the bottom of the pan.
6   Lace with coconut oil and serve hot.

*To serve 6*

## Fish Masala

*You will need :*

1    1 kg pomfret
2    1 dsp chilli powder
3    $\frac{1}{4}$ cup refined vegetable oil
4    1 tsp mustard seeds
5    $\frac{1}{2}$ cup onion paste
6    4 pieces cocum, washed and soaked in water
7    salt to taste
8    a few curry leaves
9    1 cup water

*Method :*

1    Clean the fish well in salted water and make gashes on both sides.
2    Moisten the chilli powder with a little water and keep aside.
3    Heat oil in a pan. Add mustard seeds and allow to splutter.
4    Add the ground onion paste and sauté over low heat until the oil separates and rises to the top.
5    Add chilli paste and sauté until the aroma rises.
6    Add soaked cocum, salt, curry leaves and water to make a gravy.
7    Place the fish in the gravy and cook, turning the fish, taking care not to let it crumble.
8    Serve hot.

*To serve 8*

## You will need :

1   1 kg pomfret, or fish fillets

### For the marinade :

1   1 tsp pepper powder
2   1/2 tsp turmeric powder
3   salt to taste

### For the masala paste and gravy:

1   2 tsp coriander powder
2   1/2 tsp chilli powder
3   1/2 tsp turmeric powder
4   1/2 tsp pepper powder
5   3 dsp refined vegetable oil
6   1 cup button onions, sliced
7   10 garlic cloves
8   3 green chillies, slit
9   a few curry leaves
10  1 tsp mustard seeds
11  1 cup thick coconut milk

*To serve 10*

## Meen Pollichathu
### (Fish Roasted in a Plantain Leaf)

## Method :

1   Clean fish in salted water. If using whole fish, make gashes on both sides.
2   Rub the fish well with pepper powder, turmeric powder and salt. Marinate for 1 hour.
3   Grind the coriander, chilli, turmeric and pepper powders with a little water to make masala paste.
4   In a pan, heat 2 dsp oil and sauté button onions, garlic, green chillies and curry leaves. Remove from the pan and keep aside.
5   Fry the fish lightly in the same oil and keep aside.
6   Add 1 dsp oil. Splutter mustard seeds. Add the masala paste and sauté until the aroma seems right.
7   Add fish and coconut milk.
8   Add sautéd button onions, garlic, green chillies and curry leaves. Simmer on low heat until fish is coated with gravy.
9   Wrap each fish in a piece of plantain leaf or greased foil. Tie securely and bake at 350ºF for 20 minutes. Serve hot.

# Fish with Mango

## Method :

1. Clean fish well in salted water.
2. Grind coriander powder, chilli powder, turmeric powder and garlic together.
3. Mix the fish with the ground ingredients, slit green chillies, julienned ginger and mango slices. Add 1 cup water and salt and cook.
4. When the mango pieces get soft, add ground cocount. Cook over low heat until the gravy is thick.
5. Heat oil and allow mustard seeds to splutter. Sauté onions, chillies and curry leaves. Remove from heat.
6. Mix the curry with the seasoning and serve hot.

*To serve 6*

## You will need :

1. ½ kg fish fillets, cut into small pieces
2. 2 tsp coriander powder
3. 1 tsp chilli powder
4. ½ tsp turmeric powder
5. 9 garlic cloves
6. 6 green chillies, half slit
7. 1 dsp ginger, julienned
8. 1 cup raw mango, sliced
9. 1 cup water
10. salt to taste
11. 1 cup coconut, grated and ground to a paste

## For the seasoning :

1. 2 dsp coconut oil
2. ½ tsp mustard seeds
3. 1 dsp button onions, sliced
4. 3 red chillies, quartered
5. a few curry leaves

## Fish Molee

*You will need :*

1   ¹/₂ kg fish fillets, cut into pieces
2   ¹/₄ cup refined vegetable oil
3   1 cup onion, sliced
4   1 tsp garlic, crushed
5   1 tsp ginger, crushed
6   6 green chillies, half slit
7   ¹/₂ tsp peppercorns, crushed
8   a few curry leaves
9   2 cups thin coconut milk
10  salt to taste
11  1 big tomato, cut into four
12  1 cup thick coconut milk

*Method :*

1   Clean fish well in salted water.
2   Heat oil in a pan. Sauté onion, garlic, ginger, chillies, peppercorns and curry leaves.
3   Add thin coconut milk and stir to a simmering point. Add fish pieces and salt. Cook the fish over low heat with the lid on until the gravy thickens.
4   Stir in tomato and thick coconut milk. Continue to cook over low heat for a few minutes, taking care to see that the curry does not curdle.
5   Remove from heat and serve hot.

*To serve 6*

## You will need :

1   ¹/₂ kg fish
2   1¹/₂ dsp chilli powder
3   ¹/₂ tsp pepper powder
4   ¹/₈ tsp mustard seeds
5   5 button onions
6   6 garlic cloves
7   1" ginger
8   salt to taste
9   refined vegetable oil, for frying

# Fried Fish

*Method :*

1   Clean fish well in salted water and slice.
2   Grind ingredients 2 to 7 to a fine paste. Add salt to taste.
3   Rub the fish well with the paste. Keep covered in a cool place for some time.
4   In a heavy skillet, add oil and deep fry the fish on both sides, turning gently to ensure even cooking. Serve hot.

*Note :*
The above marinade can be used for any kind of fish, but make gashes on both sides if using a whole fish.

*To serve 4*

# Meen Vevichathu
## (Red Fish Curry)

*You will need :*

1   ½ kg fish pieces
2   2 dsp chilli powder
3   ¼ tsp turmeric powder
4   ⅛ tsp fenugreek seeds
5   12 garlic cloves
6   2 tsp ginger, sliced
7   ¼ cup refined vegetable oil
8   1 tsp mustard seeds
9   2 dsp button onions, sliced
10  a few curry leaves
11  3 pieces cocum, washed and
    soaked in water
12  2 cups water
13  salt to taste

*To serve 6*

*Method :*

1.  Clean the fish pieces well in salted water.
2.  Grind ingredients 2 to 4 to a paste with 6 garlic cloves and 1 tsp ginger and keep aside.
3.  Heat oil in a pan. Splutter the mustard seeds. Add onion, remaining garlic, ginger and curry leaves. Keep stirring and when it turns slightly brown drain from oil and keep aside.
4.  In the same oil, stir in the ground masala, and fry until the aroma rises. Add the soaked cocum and 2 cups water. Add salt to taste.
5.  Transfer this into an earthenware vessel and simmer. Gently ladle in the fish pieces and the sautéd ingredients.
6.  Cook half covered, till it boils.
7.  Remove the lid and allow to simmer on low heat till the gravy thickens and the fish is cooked.

# Mathi Vattichathu
## (Sardines cooked Dry)

*You will need :*

1   ¹/₂ kg sardines

*To serve 5*

*For the masala :*

1   10 red chillies
2   ¹/₈ tsp fenugreek seeds
3   8 peppercorns
4   ¹/₂ tsp turmeric powder
5   ¹/₂ cup button onions, sliced
6   ¹/₂ dsp ginger, julienned
7   2 dsp garlic cloves, crushed/sliced/chopped
8   a few curry leaves
9   ¹/₂ cup coconut oil or any refined vegetable oil
10  3 pieces cocum, washed, soaked and shredded in water
11  salt to taste
12  ¹/₂ cup water

*Method :*

1   Clean the sardines in salted water. Make a slit on the side and remove the inside portion of each fish. Make gashes on both sides of the fish.
2   Coarsely grind ingredients 1 to 8 and keep aside.
3   Mix the ground ingredients with coconut oil, shredded cocum and salt.
4   Grease an earthenware vessel with coconut oil and layer the fish and the mixed masala alternately; finish with a layer of masala on top.
5   Add water to cook the fish and bring to boil.
6   Simmer over low heat till dry. Serve hot.

# Masala Pomfret

*You will need :*

1. 1/2 kg pomfret, cleaned and gashed for stuffing

*For the marinade :*

1. 9 red chillies
2. 1/8 tsp pepper powder
3. 1/8 tsp cumin seeds
4. 1/8 tsp fenugreek seeds
5. 1/8 tsp mustard seeds
6. 1/4 tsp turmeric powder
7. 4 garlic cloves
8. 1/2" ginger
9. 5 button onions
10. salt to taste
11. 1 dsp lime juice

*To serve 5*

*For the stuffing :*

1. 2 dsp refined vegetable oil
2. 1 cup onion, sliced
3. 1/4 cup green chillies, chopped
4. 1/2 tsp ginger, chopped
5. 2 dsp tomato, chopped
6. salt to taste
7. 1/8 tsp sugar
8. white of one egg
9. refined vegetable oil for frying

*Method :*

1. Grind the ingredients for the marinade.
2. Rub 2 dsp marinade evenly all over the fish and keep covered in a cool place for 2-3 hours.
3. Heat oil in a pan and fry onions, green chillies and ginger; fry till the onions are light brown in colour. Add tomatoes and sauté until dry.
4. Add salt and sugar and mix well. Stuff the fish with this mixture. Seal the opening with beaten egg-white.
5. Heat oil in a skillet and fry the fish on both sides over low heat. Serve hot.

*You will need :*

1   ½ kg prawns

*For the masala :*

1   1 tsp chilli powder
2   1 tsp coriander powder
3   ⅛ tsp pepper powder
4   10 button onions
5   2" ginger
6   10 garlic cloves
7   3 pieces cocum, washed and
     soaked in water
8   8-10 curry leaves
9   2 cups water
10  salt to taste
11  1 tsp ginger, julienned

*Prawn Oolarthiathu*

*For the seasoning :*

1   ½ cup coconut oil or
     any refined vegetable
     oil
2   1 tsp mustard seeds
3   2 cups onion, sliced
4   a few curry leaves


*To serve 5*

*Method :*

1   Wash prawns, shell and devein.
2   Coarsely grind ingredients 1 to 6.
3   In an earthernware vessel, mix the ground ingredients with cocum, a few of the
     curry leaves, water and salt.
4   Immerse and cook prawns until soft with 1 tsp ginger. When the curry is almost
     dry, remove from fire.
5   Heat the oil in a pan. Splutter the mustard seeds, add the sliced onions and fry till
     brown. Add the remaining curry leaves.
6   Add the prawn mixture and fry well. Remove from fire and serve hot.

## Prawn Pappas

### Method :

1 Wash the prawns well. Shell and devein. Parboil the prawns in salt and water till dry and keep aside.

2 Grind ingredients 4 to 8 and keep aside.

3 Heat oil in a pan. Splutter mustard seeds.

4 Add ingredients 11 to 16 and fry till the onions turn golden in colour.

5 Add the masala paste and fry over low heat till an aroma rises.

6 Add cocum and fry again.

7 Add thin coconut milk and bring to a simmering point.

8 Ladle in the cooked prawns. Add salt to taste. Cook over low heat till the gravy thickens.

9 Add thick coconut milk. Cook for a few minutes and remove from heat. Serve hot.

*To serve 4*

### You will need :

1 ¹/₂ kg prawns
2 1 cup water
3 salt to taste
4 1 dsp coriander powder
5 ¹/₂ tsp chilli powder
6 ¹/₄ tsp turmeric powder
7 ¹/₄ tsp pepper powder
8 4 button onions
9 ¹/₄ cup refined vegetable oil
10 1 tsp mustard seeds
11 ¹/₈ tsp fenugreek seeds
12 1 cup onion, sliced
13 1 tsp ginger, julienned
14 12 garlic cloves
15 3 green chillies, half slit
16 a few curry leaves
17 4 pieces cocum, washed and soaked in water
18 2 cups thin coconut milk
19 ¹/₂ cup thick coconut milk

# Vegetables

1　Parippu

2　Sambar (with Sambar Powder)

3　Tomato Rasam

4　Kaalan

5　Avial

6　Olan

7　Erissery

8　Idichakka Thoran (Tender Jackfruit)

9　Cheera Thoran (Spinach)

10　Kanji Payar Thoran (Whole Green Beans)

11　Pineapple Pachadi

12　Theeyal

13　Ripe Mango Curry

14　Okra Curry

15　Masala Kadala

16　Kappa Puratiyathu (Mashed Tapioca)

17　Mezhukku Puratiyathu

18　Okra Fry

19　Kaya Warathathu (Banana Fry)

20　Deep Fried Bitter Gourd

21　Kachiamoru (Spiced Buttermilk)

# Parippu

*You will need :*

1.  1 cup husked green beans
2.  3 cups water
3.  ¼ tsp chilli powder
4.  4 garlic cloves
5.  ¼ tsp cumin seeds
6.  ¼ tsp turmeric powder
7.  1 cup coconut, grated

*Method :*

1.  Lightly roast beans in a thick-bottomed skillet on a slow fire without permitting the colour of the beans to change. Then cook the green beans in 3 cups water.
2.  Grind ingredients 3 to 7 to a fine paste. Mix the paste in a little water and add to the cooked beans. Add salt to taste. Bring to boil and remove from fire.
3.  In a mixture of oil and ghee, fry mustard seeds, button onions, curry leaves and chillies and add to the curry. Serve hot.

*For the seasoning :*

1.  2 dsp refined vegetable oil
2.  1 dsp ghee
3.  1 tsp mustard seeds
4.  2 tsp button onions, sliced in rounds
5.  a few curry leaves
6.  2 dry red chillies, quartered
7.  salt to taste

*To serve 6*

# Sambar (with Sambar Powder)

### You will need :

1  1 cup pigeon peas
2  1 tsp turmeric powder
3  5 $\frac{1}{2}$ cups water
4  tamarind, the size of a lime
5  $\frac{1}{4}$ kg mixed vegetables
   (brinjal, cucumber, drumstick,
   potato, onion), cut into pieces
6  4 green chillies, half slit
7  salt to taste
8  2 dsp sambar powder

### For the seasoning :

1  1 dsp refined vegetable oil
2  $\frac{1}{2}$ tsp mustard seeds
3  1 dsp onion, chopped
4  1 dry red chilli, halved
5  a few curry leaves
6  a few coriander leaves

### For the sambar powder :

1  1 dsp gingelly oil
2  $\frac{1}{2}$ tsp asafoetida powder
3  1 tsp fenugreek seeds
4  12 dry red chillies
5  2 dsp coriander seeds

### To prepare the sambar powder :

1  Heat the gingelly oil. Roast all the
   ingredients one by one. Mix
   together and powder finely. Store
   in an airtight tin.

### Method :

1  Cook the washed pigeon peas
   with turmeric powder in 3 cups
   water.
2  Soak tamarind in $\frac{1}{2}$ cup water.
3  Cook vegetables in 2 cups water.
   When the vegetables are cooked,
   strain and pour in the tamarind
   extract and the sambar powder.
4  Allow it to boil for 10 minutes.
   Remove from fire.
5.  Heat oil. Season the sambar with
   mustard seeds, onion, red chilli
   and curry leaves. Garnish with
   coriander leaves.

*To serve 6*

# Tomato Rasam

*You will need :*

1   ¹/₄ cup pigeon peas
2   4 cups water
3   4 garlic cloves
4   ¹/₂ tsp cumin seeds
5   1 tsp ginger, sliced
6   ¹/₄ tsp peppercorns
7   4 tomatoes, medium sized,
     cut into large pieces
8   ¹/₂ tsp asafoetida powder
9   ¹/₂ tsp chilli powder
10  ¹/₂ tsp coriander powder
11  salt to taste
12  juice of half a lime

*For the seasoning :*

1   1 dsp refined vegetable oil
2   ¹/₂ tsp mustard seeds
3   1 tsp husked black beans
4   2 red chillies, halved
5   2 dsp coriander leaves

*Method :*

1   Cook the pigeon peas in 4 cups
    water, until soft. Crush garlic, cumin
    seeds, ginger and peppercorns and
    add. Put in tomatoes, asafoetida,
    chilli and coriander powders and
    salt. When it boils, remove from the
    fire and strain. Add lime juice
    according to taste.

2   Heat oil and splutter mustard seeds.
    Add black beans, chillies and
    coriander leaves and fry lightly. Pour
    over rasam.

*To serve 8*

*Kaalan*

**You will need :**

1   1 cup raw banana, diced
2   6 green chillies, slit
3   $1/2$ tsp chilli powder
4   $1/4$ tsp turmeric powder
5   salt to taste
6   1 cup coconut, grated
7   $1/4$ tsp cumin seeds
8   4 cups curd, lightly beaten

**For the seasoning :**

1   2 dsp refined vegetable oil
2   1 tsp mustard seeds
3   $1/8$ tsp fenugreek seeds
4   3 dry red chillies, halved
5   a few curry leaves

**Method :**

1   Cook the banana pieces in a cup of water, with green chillies, chilli powder and turmeric powder. Add salt to taste.

2   Grind grated coconut and cumin seeds to a fine paste. Add this paste to the cooked banana. Mix well and allow to boil once. Lower the heat and add the beaten curd at once, stirring all the time. Take care it does not curdle. Remove from fire.

3   Heat another pan with 2 dsp oil. Splutter mustard seeds, add fenugreek seeds, red chillies and curry leaves and fry lightly. Pour over the curry.

**Variation :**

Kaalan can also be made with pineapple instead of banana.

*To serve 6*

*Avial*

## You will need :

1  ¹/₂ kg mixed vegetables,
   sliced into 1" pieces lengthwise
   (drumstick, cucumber, string beans,
   brinjal, yam, raw banana, snake gourd)
2  ¹/₂ tsp chilli powder
3  ¹/₃ tsp turmeric powder
4  salt to taste
5  2 dsp coconut oil
6  8 green chillies, half slit
7  tamarind pulp to taste, or
   ¹/₂ raw mango, sliced
8  1 cup coconut, grated
9  ¹/₄ tsp cumin seeds
10 4 button onions
11 a few curry leaves

## Method :

1  To the sliced vegetables add chilli powder, turmeric powder, salt and 1 dsp coconut oil. Add slit green chillies. Cook on low flame, without water.
2  Once the vegetables are cooked, add the tamarind pulp or the raw mango and allow it to boil once.
3  Grind the grated coconut coarsely, with cumin seeds and button onions.
4  Mix the coarsely ground ingredients to the vegetables. Allow to cook over low heat till it blends well.
5  Remove from heat, add the curry leaves and lace with 1 dsp coconut oil. Serve hot.

*To serve 6*

# Olan

*You will need :*

1. ¹/₂ cup black-eyed beans
2. 2 ¹/₂ cups water
3. 2 cups ash gourd, diced
4. 6 green chillies, half slit
5. salt to taste
6. 1 cup thick coconut milk
7. a few curry leaves
8. 1 dsp coconut oil

*Method :*

1. Pressure cook the black-eyed beans in 1¹/₂ cups water and keep aside.
2. Cook the ash gourd with green chillies, salt and 1 cup water.
3. Add the cooked beans and allow to simmer for a while. Add coconut milk and curry leaves. Remove from heat.
4. Finally lace with coconut oil. Serve hot.

*To serve 6*

Erissery

*You will need :*

1  $^1/_4$ cup black-eyed beans
2  2 cups water
3  2 cups pumpkin, finely chopped
4  $^1/_2$ cup coconut, grated
5  $^1/_2$ tsp turmeric powder
6  $^1/_2$ tsp chilli powder
7  3 garlic gloves
8  salt to taste

*For the seasoning :*

1  2 dsp coconut oil
2  1 tsp mustard seeds
3  2 dsp onion, chopped
4  a few curry leaves
5  2 dry red chillies, halved
6  2 dsp coconut, grated

*Method :*

1  Cook the washed beans in 2 cups water. Add the chopped pumpkin and cook.
2  Coarsely grind ingredients 4 to 7 and add to the cooked vegetable. Mix well and add salt.
3  Heat oil, splutter mustard seeds. Toss in the chopped onion, curry leaves and red chillies.
4  Add grated coconut and sauté until the coconut is lightly browned. Stir this seasoning into the curry. Serve hot.

*To serve 4*

# Idichakka Thoran
## (Tender Jackfruit)

*You will need :*

1  3 cups tender jackfruit, diced
2  ¼ tsp turmeric powder
3  salt to taste
4  1 cup water
5  1 cup coconut, grated
6  ¼ tsp cumin seeds
7  ½ tsp chilli powder
8  2 garlic cloves

*For the seasoning :*

1  2 dsp refined vegetable oil
2  ½ tsp mustard seeds
3  1 tsp rice
4  2 dry red chillies, halved
5  a few curry leaves

*Method :*

1  Place the diced jackfruit in a pan with a pinch of turmeric and salt to taste. Add 1 cup water and cook till done.
2  Drain the cooked jackfruit, crush with a pestle and shred.
3  Coarsely grind the grated coconut, cumin seeds, chilli powder and garlic.
4  Heat oil and allow mustard seeds and rice to splutter. Add red chillies and curry leaves. Sauté till brown.
5  Add the coarsely ground ingredients to the jackfruit and sauté again. Allow the mixture to dry out completely before removing from heat. Serve hot.

*To serve 6*

## Cheera Thoran
### (Spinach)

**You will need :**

1   2 garlic cloves
2   $1/4$ tsp turmeric powder
3   $1/5$ tsp chilli powder
4   1 cup coconut, grated
5   2 dsp refined vegetable oil
6   $1/2$ tsp mustard seeds
7   2 dry red chillies, halved
8   a few curry leaves
9   3 cups spinach, finely chopped
10  1 tsp green chilli, finely chopped
11  salt to taste

**Method :**

1   Grind garlic, turmeric powder, chilli powder and coconut coarsely.
2   Heat oil and splutter mustard seeds. Add red chillies and curry leaves. Put in the chopped spinach and green chilli. Sprinkle a little water and salt. Cover the pan. When steam rises, ladle the ground masala into the centre and cover it with spinach. Close the pan and continue cooking till it steams again. Open and stir gently till the water is absorbed. Serve hot.

*Variation :*

Cabbage, string beans, raw papaya and carrots can also be used instead of spinach.

*To serve 4*

# Kanji Payar Thoran
## (Whole Green Beans)

**You will need :**

1. 1 cup whole green beans
2. 3 cups water
3. $1/8$ tsp cumin seeds
4. $1/4$ tsp turmeric powder
5. 3 garlic cloves
6. 1 green chilli
7. 1 cup coconut, grated
8. salt to taste

**For the seasoning :**

1. 2 dsp refined vegetable oil
2. $1/2$ tsp mustard seeds
3. 1 dry red chilli, broken into 3 pieces
4. a few curry leaves

*To serve 6*

**Method :**

1. The green beans may be lightly roasted for two minutes before cooking. This prevents it from getting mashed.
2. Wash and clean the beans and cook covered in 3 cups boiling water. When it starts to boil, half open the pan and cook till the water is almost absorbed.
3. Grind together cumin seeds and turmeric powder. Crush garlic, green chilli and grated coconut. Mix the ground ingredients together.
4. Before all the water evaporates ladle the ground ingredients into the centre of the cooked beans and cover it with some of the beans. When steam escapes, stir gently using the handle of the ladle and let it dry without getting mashed. Add salt and mix well.
5. Heat oil in a pan and splutter mustard seeds. Add chilli and curry leaves and fry lightly. Add to the thoran.

## Pineapple Pachadi

*Method :*

1   Cook pineapple with green chillies, ginger, salt and ¹/₂ cup water.

2   Grind coconut and red chillies to a paste. Add crushed mustard seeds.

3   Mix the ground ingredients with the cooked pineapple. Allow it to boil once and remove from fire. Add beaten curd and mix well.

4   Heat oil in a pan and splutter mustard seeds. Add red chillies and curry leaves.

5   Pour the seasoning over the cooked pineapple. Mix well.

*To serve 6*

*You will need :*

1   2 cups ripe pineapple, chopped
2   2 green chillies, half slit
3   1" ginger, sliced
4   salt to taste
5   ¹/₂ cup water
6   1 cup coconut, grated
7   2 dry red chillies
8   1 tsp mustard seeds, crushed
9   ¹/₂ cup curd, beaten

*For the seasoning :*

1   2 dsp refined vegetable oil
2   ¹/₂ tsp mustard seeds
3   3 dry red chillies, halved
4   a few curry leaves

*Theeyal*

*You will need :*

1  2 cups coconut, grated
2  4 dry red chillies
3  1 tsp coriander seeds
4  2 dsp button onions, sliced
5  1 dsp refined vegetable oil
6  ¼ tsp turmeric powder
7  250 gms brinjal,
    sliced 1" lengthwise
8  6 green chillies, slit
9  a few curry leaves
10  tamarind, the size of a lime,
    soaked in 1 cup water
11  ½ cup water
12  salt to taste

*For the seasoning :*

1  1 dsp coconut oil
2  ¼ tsp mustard seeds
3  2 dry red chillies, halved
4  3 button onions, sliced

*Method :*

1  In a deep pan, lightly roast the grated coconut, red chillies, coriander seeds and 1 dsp button onions. Grind all the roasted ingredients to a fine paste.

2  In the same pan, heat 1 tsp oil and add turmeric powder. Sauté and add the brinjal pieces, 1 dsp button onions and green chillies.

3  Strain and add tamarind water and the ground masala. Add water and salt to taste and cook over low heat till the gravy thickens.

4  In a small saucepan, heat oil and allow mustard seeds to splutter. Add the halved red chillies and the sliced button onions and pour over the curry.

5  Serve hot.

*To serve 4*

# Ripe Mango Curry

*You will need :*

1   $^1/_2$ kg small ripe mangoes
2   1 cup water
3   4 green chillies, slit
4   1 tsp chilli powder
5   $^1/_2$ tsp turmeric powder
6   a few curry leaves
7   salt to taste
8   $^1/_2$ tsp cumin powder
9   $^1/_2$ cup coconut milk

*For the seasoning :*

1   2 dsp refined vegetable oil
2   1 tsp mustard seeds
3   2 dry red chillies, halved

*Method :*

1   Remove skin from mangoes, add 1 cup water and cook with green chillies, chilli powder, turmeric powder, curry leaves and salt.
2   Add cumin powder to coconut milk. When the mango mixture cools, add the coconut milk and mix well.
3   Heat oil in a pan and splutter the mustard seeds. Add red chillies and pour into the curry.
4   Serve hot.

*To serve 4*

*Okra Curry*

*You will need :*

1 1 tsp coriander powder
2 ¼ tsp chilli powder
3 ¼ tsp turmeric powder
4 ¼ tsp pepper powder
5 ¼ tsp aniseed
6 1" cinnamon
7 2 cardamom pods
8 4 cloves
9 ¼ cup refined vegetable oil
10 2 cups okra,
    sliced 1" lengthwise
11 ½ cup onion, sliced
12 1 tsp ginger, julienned
13 5 green chillies, half slit
14 a few curry leaves
15 1½ cups thin coconut milk
16 salt to taste
17 lime juice to taste
18 ½ cup thick coconut milk

*Method :*

1 Grind ingredients 1 to 8 to a fine paste.
2 Heat oil in a pan and sauté the sliced okra. Keep aside.
3 In the same pan, add the onion, ginger, green chillies and curry leaves.
4 Add the ground paste and sauté for a while. When the oil separates, pour in the thin coconut milk and bring to boil.
5 Add the sautéd okra, salt and lime juice and simmer till the gravy thickens.
6 Gently add the thick coconut milk. Mix well and remove from heat.

*To serve 4*

## Masala Kadala

*You will need :*

1  2 cups whole Bengal gram
2  4 1/2 cups water
3  salt to taste
4  1 1/2 cups refined vegetable oil
5  1 1/2 cups onion, finely sliced
6  1/2 cup potato, cubed
7  1/2 cup bread,
   cubed like croutons
8  6 green chillies, half slit
9  2 large tomatoes,
   each cut into 8 pieces
10  1/2 tsp sugar
11  1/2 tsp mustard seeds
12  1 dsp chilli powder
13  1 dsp coriander powder
14  1/4 tsp turmeric powder
15  a few coriander leaves
16  1 lime

*Method :*

1  Wash and soak Bengal gram in 2 cups water overnight. Pressure cook with salt in 2 1/2 cups water for 40 minutes.

2  Heat 1 cup oil. Add 1 cup sliced onion. Fry well, drain and keep aside. Fry and drain potato cubes. Fry cubes of bread; drain and keep aside. Sauté green chillies and tomatoes. Sprinkle salt and sugar on all the above ingredients. Remove from fire.

3  Take another pan and heat 1/2 cup oil. Splutter mustard seeds. Add 1/2 cup onion and fry till brown. Mix the chilli, coriander and turmeric powders in a little water and make into a paste. Lower the flame and add the paste to the pan. Add the cooked Bengal gram and mix gently. Spread the curry on a large, flat dish and garnish with the fried onion, potato, green chilli, tomato and cubes of bread. Coriander leaves and quartered lime may also be used to garnish the dish.

*To serve 6*

# Kappa Puratiyathu
## (Mashed Tapioca)

*You will need :*

1   1 kg tapioca
2   ¹/₂ tsp chilli powder
3   1 cup coconut, grated
4   ¹/₄ tsp turmeric powder
5   4 garlic cloves
6   ¹/₄ tsp cumin seeds
7   salt to taste

*For the seasoning :*

1   2 dsp refined vegetable oil
2   ¹/₂ tsp mustard seeds
3   2 dsp button onions, chopped
4   2 dry red chillies, halved
5   a few curry leaves
6   2 dsp coconut, grated (optional)

*Method :*

1   Peel and chop the tapioca into small pieces. Allow it to cook in plenty of water. Drain and keep aside.
2   Coarsely grind the chilli powder, coconut, turmeric powder, garlic and cumin seeds.
3   Place the tapioca in a deep pan. Scoop out some from the centre and place the ground ingredients in the space created. Add salt to taste and cover with the scooped out tapioca. Mash the tapioca.
4   Cover and cook over low heat.
5   Heat oil. Splutter mustard seeds. Add button onions, red chillies, curry leaves and grated coconut. Sauté till brown.
6   Add the seasoning to the tapioca and mix well. Serve hot.

*To serve 5*

# Mezhukku Puratiyathu

*You will need :*

1   2 cups yam, peeled and chopped into 1" pieces
2   4 cups water
3   salt to taste
4   2 dsp button onions
5   3 dry red chillies
6   a few peppercorns
7   6 garlic cloves
8   a few curry leaves
9   2 dsp refined vegetable oil

*Method :*

1   Wash the yam pieces twice, drain and cook in 4 cups boiling water. Add salt after the yam is cooked. Drain off the excess water.
2   Crush ingredients 4 to 8. Heat oil in a pan. Add the crushed ingredients. Sauté well.
3   Add the cooked yam pieces and mix gently. When the pieces are well coated, remove from heat. Serve hot.

*Variation :*

Vegetables like green plantain or beans can also be used instead of yam.

*To serve 5*

Okra Fry

You will need :

1   250 gms okra
2   salt to taste
3   1 tsp chilli powder
4   ¹/₂ tsp asafoetida powder
5   2 dsp gram flour
6   250 gms refined vegetable oil

Method :

1   Slit the okra into thin pieces lengthwise.
    Marinate with salt, chilli powder and
    asafoetida powder for five minutes.
    Sprinkle gram flour and toss. Deep fry
    in hot oil.
2   Serve hot.

To serve 6

# Kaya Warathathu
## (Banana Fry)

*You will need :*

1   ¹/₂ kg banana, not too mature
2   coconut oil for frying
3   salt to taste

*Method :*

1   Pare the bananas, wash and dry well.
2   Slice into thin, round sections of even thickness.
3   Deep fry the slices in hot oil till crisp.
4   Sprinkle a little salt water in the oil. Stir again so that the salt is evenly absorbed by the chips. When the spluttering subsides, remove the chips from the oil, place in a strainer and let the oil drain away.
5   When cool, store in airtight containers to keep fresh and crisp.

*To serve 6*

## Deep Fried Bitter Gourd

*You will need :*

1   1/2 kg bitter gourd
2   1 tsp chilli powder
3   6 green chillies, slit
4   1/2 cup coconut bits (optional)
5   salt to taste
6   1/2 cup refined vegetable oil
7   1/2 cup onion, sliced thin and long

*Method :*

1   Slit open the bitter gourd. Remove the seeds and cut into thin, round slices.
2   Mix with chilli powder, green chillies, coconut bits and salt.
3   Squeeze out the excess water.
4   Heat the oil, fry the sliced onion and keep aside.
5   Add a little more oil if required and fry the bitter gourd along with green chillies and coconut bits. When crisp, drain.
6   Mix the onion with the bitter gourd and serve.

*To serve 6*

# Kachiamoru
## (Spiced Buttermilk)

*You will need :*

1   6 cups fresh buttermilk (not sour)
2   ¼ tsp turmeric powder
3   a few curry leaves
4   salt to taste
5   1 cup coconut, grated
6   ¼ tsp chilli powder
7   3 button onions
8   ¼ tsp cumin seeds

*For the seasoning :*

1   1 dsp refined vegetable oil
2   ¼ tsp mustard seeds
3   ¼ tsp fenugreek seeds
4   2 dry red chillies, halved

*Method :*

1   Mix into the buttermilk turmeric powder, curry leaves and salt. Grind ingredients 5 to 8 and add. Heat the mixture over a low flame, stirring continuously. When the first bubble appears, remove from flame and continue stirring till it cools.

2   Heat oil. Splutter mustard seeds, add fenugreek seeds and red chillies and fry lightly. Cool and add to buttermilk.

*To serve 8*

# Rice

1    Mutton Biriyani

2    Coconut Rice

3    Lime Rice

4    Ghee Rice

# Mutton Biriyani

*You will need :*

1   Mutton kurma
    (See recipe on p. 4)
2   salt to taste
3   3 litres (12 cups) water
4   ¹/₂ kg basmati rice,
    soaked in water for 15 minutes
5   ¹/₂ cup ghee
6   ¹/₂ cup onion, finely sliced
7   ¹/₄ cup cashewnuts
8   ¹/₄ cup raisins

*To serve 4*

*Method :*

1   Keep the mutton kurma ready. Add salt in 12 cups boiling water, cook the soaked rice and drain.

2   Heat ghee and fry onions until golden. Remove and in the same pan fry the cashewnuts and raisins separately. Remove and keep aside.

3   Grease a heavy-bottomed vessel with ghee and arrange rice at the bottom. Over it arrange pieces of meat from the kurma. Repeat in layers. Then pour the gravy over and add a final layer of rice. Cover the rice with a damp cloth and place a lid over it.

4   Bake in a warm oven at 325°F for half an hour. Serve hot, garnished with fried onions, cashewnuts and raisins.

# Coconut Rice

*You will need :*

1. ¹/₄ cup ghee
2. 2 cups basmati rice, soaked in water for 15 minutes
3. 5 cups coconut milk
4. salt to taste
5. ¹/₄ cup coconut, grated

*Method :*

1. Heat the ghee in a heavy-bottomed vessel. Stir fry the rice in it till slightly brown. Add coconut milk and bring to boil. Lower the flame and cook till done. Add salt and stand over a very slow fire till all the water is absorbed.
2. Roast grated coconut lightly and sprinkle over hot rice before serving.

*To serve 4*

# Lime Rice

## You will need :

1   2 cups rice
2   2 dsp ghee
3   salt to taste
4   $1/2$ tsp sugar
5   3 dsp lime juice
6   3 dsp gingelly oil
7   $1/2$ tsp mustard seeds
8   2 dsp Bengal gram
9   3 dry red chillies, halved
10  $1/2$ tsp turmeric powder
11  $1/2$ dsp green chillies, chopped

## For the garnish :

1   $1/2$ cup onion, finely sliced
2   2 dsp raisins
3   $1/2$ cup potato, julienned
4   $1/4$ cup refined vegetable oil
5   a few coriander leaves

## Method :

1   Cook the rice. Stir in the ghee, salt, sugar and lime juice.
2   Heat the gingelly oil and splutter mustard seeds. Add Bengal gram, red chillies, turmeric powder and green chillies. Add this to the rice and mix well.
3   Garnish with sliced onion, raisins and potato juliennes fried well in $1/4$ cup oil. Sprinkle coriander leaves before serving.

*To serve 4*

## Ghee Rice

*You will need :*

1  2 cups basmati rice, soaked in water for 15 minutes
2  ¹/₂ cup ghee
3  1 cup onion, finely sliced
4  ¹/₄ cup raisins
5  ¹/₄ cup cashewnut slivers
6  4 sticks cinnamon, 1" each
7  4 cardamom pods
8  4 cloves
9  5 cups water
10 salt to taste

*To serve 4*

*Method :*

1  Clean, wash and drain the rice.
2  Heat ghee and fry half the onion till golden brown. Drain and store in an airtight container to retain crispness. Fry raisins and cashewnuts separately in the remaining ghee. Set aside.
3  In the same vessel, sauté the spices along with the rest of the onion. Add rice and fry well, taking care not to crumble the grains.
4  Add 5 cups boiling water to the rice and cook over a low flame. When the water begins to boil again, add salt, cover and cook till all the water is absorbed.
5  Garnish with fried onion, cashewnuts and raisins before serving.

# Pickles

1    Tender Mango Pickle

2    Special Mango Pickle

3    Lime Pickle

4    Ginger Curry

# Tender Mango Pickle

## To salt the mangoes :

1. 6 kg tender green mangoes
2. salt to taste
3. approximately 6 litres water

### Method :

1. Wash the mangoes well and wipe dry.
2. Dissolve the salt in the water, which should be just sufficient to immerse the mangoes.
3. Bring to boil. Cool and strain.
4. Place the mangoes in a large, dry jar.
5. Stir the salt solution and pour over the mangoes.
6. Close the jar with an airtight lid and seal with wax. Alternatively, tie a soft cloth around the lid and seal with cellophane tape.
7. Preserve for two weeks before using for pickle.

### Note :

Store in a 10 litre jar.

## For the pickle:

1. 1 kg salted tender mangoes
2. $1/2$ cup chilli powder
3. $1/4$ cup mustard seeds
4. $1/2$ tsp asafoetida
5. $1/2$ cup gingelly oil

### Method :

1. Ladle $1^1/2$ cups brine from the jar in which the mangoes are preserved, into a bowl.
2. Soak the chilli powder in a little brine.
3. Powder the mustard seeds and asafoetida, after lightly frying in gingelly oil.
4. Mix the soaked chilli powder and the powdered ingredients and grind to a paste. Mix in the remaining brine.
5. Add this to the salted mangoes.

### Note :

The liquid should cover the mangoes. If more liquid is required, use the brine from the salted mangoes, adding more chilli powder to it, if necessary.

## Special Mango Pickle

*You will need :*

1   4 cups green mango, lighty
    pared and diced
2   salt to taste
3   ¼ cup gingelly oil
4   ¼ tsp mustard powder
5   ¼ tsp turmeric powder
6   ½ cup chilli powder
7   1 tsp asafoetida powder
8   ¼ tsp fenugreek powder
9   a few curry leaves
10  2 cups water, boiled and cooled

*Method :*

1   Toss the diced mango in salt. Set aside for two hours.
2   Heat the gingelly oil and fry the mustard, turmeric, chilli, asafoetida and fenugreek
    powders and curry leaves over a moderate flame. Add the water and bring to boil.
3   Remove from fire and cool.
4   Stir in the marinated mango. Mix well and bottle.

Lime Pickle

## You will need :

1   25 ripe limes
2   ¹/₂ cup gingelly oil
3   2 tsp mustard seeds
4   1 tsp fenugreek seeds
5   1 tsp turmeric powder
6   ¹/₂ cup garlic cloves
7   2 dsp ginger, julienned
8   18 green chillies, slit with stalks
9   1 tsp asafoetida powder
10  3 dsp chilli powder
11  ³/₄ cup salt

## Method :

1   Steam lime for 5 minutes. Spread on a tray to cool and wipe dry.
2   Heat oil, splutter mustard seeds and add fenugreek seeds. Lower the flame and add turmeric powder.
4   Add the garlic, ginger and green chillies and sauté till the colour changes.
5   Remove from fire and add asafoetida and chilli powders while still hot. Mix well, cool and then add the salt.
6   Cut each lime into 8 pieces.
7   Pack the lime slices in a clean dry jar, alternating each layer with a layer of the sautéd ingredients. Use after one week.

## Ginger Curry

### You will need :

1   6 1"ginger cubes
2   1 tsp rice flour
3   1/2 cup gingelly oil
4   2 green chillies
5   1 dsp coriander seeds
6   8 dry red chillies
7   1/4 tsp fenugreek seeds
8   tamarind, the size of a lime, soaked in 1 cup water
9   1 tsp  sugar or jaggery
10  salt to taste

### For the seasoning :

1   1 dsp gingelly oil
2   1/8 tsp mustard seeds
3   2 dry red chillies, halved
4   a few curry leaves

### Method :

1   Crush ginger and squeeze out juice.
2   Dredge the ginger shreds in the rice flour and fry in 1/4 cup gingelly oil with green chillies. Remove and grind coarsely. Set aside.
3   Over a low flame, roast the coriander seeds, red chillies and fenugreek in 1/2 dsp gingelly oil. Grind to a smooth paste.
4   Extract juice from the tamarind. Add to the shredded fried ginger, ground masala and salt.
5   Keep on fire and bring to boil. Simmer till the gravy thickens. Then add the jaggery or sugar and simmer for a few minutes more.
7   Fry the ingredients for the seasoning in  1 dsp. hot oil and add to the gravy.

# Desserts

1. Paal Ada Pradhaman
2. Vermicelli Payasam
3. Parippu Payasam
4. Tender Coconut Pudding

# Paal Ada Pradhaman

*You will need :*

1   250 gms rice flour
2   2 litres milk
3   2 cups water
4   2 $\frac{1}{2}$ cups sugar
5   1 $\frac{1}{2}$ dsp butter
6   $\frac{1}{2}$ tsp cardamon powder
7   $\frac{1}{4}$ cup cashewnuts, fried in ghee/butter
8   $\frac{1}{4}$ cup raisins, fried in ghee/butter

*Method :*

1   Add the rice flour to 2 cups milk and mix well to make a soft batter.
2   Pour spoonfuls of the batter on to 6" square banana leaves and swirl to spread evenly.
3   Roll up the leaves and drop them into boiling water.
4   Cook for 10 minutes and remove from the water.
5   Cool and unroll the leaves. Drop the 'ada' (steamed pancakes) into a large vessel.
6   Chop the ada into small pieces.
7   Heat butter in a large heavy-bottomed vessel and lightly sauté the ada in it.
8   Mix the milk, water and sugar together. Add gradually to the sautéd ada and cook well, stirring all the time till it thickens.
9   Add the powdered cardamom, cashewnuts and raisins. Stir well. Serve hot.

## Vermicelli Payasam

*You will need :*

1   2 dsp ghee
2   2 dsp cashewnuts, halved
3   1 dsp raisins
4   200 gms vermicelli
5   4 cups water
6   2 litres milk
7   1 cup sugar
8.  $\frac{1}{4}$ tsp cardamom powder

*Method :*

1   Heat ghee and lightly fry the cashewnuts and raisins. Set aside.
2   Grease a skillet with ghee and fry the vermicelli in it, till light brown.
3   Boil the water in a pan and add the vermicelli to it.
4   When half the water is absorbed, add the milk and sugar and simmer.
5   Stir in cardamom powder. Sprinkle the fried cashewnuts and raisins over the payasam. Remove from fire and serve hot.

*To serve 6*

## Parippu payasam

### You will need :

1.  2 coconuts, grated
2.  2 cups husked green beans
3.  8 ¹/₂ cups water
4.  ¹/₄ cup sago
5.  ¹/₂ cup coconut slivers
6.  4 dsp ghee
7.  ¹/₂ kg jaggery
8.  ¹/₂ tsp dried ginger powder or ³/₄ tsp cardamom powder
9.  ¹/₂ tsp cumin powder

### Method :

1.  Extract 2 cups thick milk from the grated coconut. Add water to the residue and extract another 6 cups.
2.  Roast the green beans in a heavy skillet till an aroma rises.
3.  Cook the beans in five cups water till the beans are soft and the water has been absorbed.
4.  Boil 3 cups water. Add sago and cook till transparent. Drain off the water and wash in cold water. Strain and keep aside.
5.  Fry the coconut slivers in 1 dsp ghee. Keep aside.
6.  Add ¹/₂ cup water to the jaggery and melt over low heat. Strain into beans and cook, stirring in the remaining ghee.
5.  Simmer gently, and as it thickens add the second extract (6 cups) of coconut milk and the sago.
6.  When done, add the powdered spices mixed in the first extract of coconut milk (2 cups). Do not allow to boil. Into this, add the coconut slivers.
7.  Stir well and remove from fire.

*To serve 6*

## Tender Coconut Pudding

*You will need :*

1. 10 gms China grass
2. 1 cup water
3. 1 cup tender coconut water
4. 1 tin condensed milk
5. 2 tins milk
6. 5 dsp sugar
7. 1 cup thin scrapings of tender coconut
8. $^1/_4$ cup coconut, finely grated

*Method :*

1. Soak China grass in 1 cup water and dissolve over low flame. Remove from heat.
2. Add the tender coconut water.
3. In another pan, dissolve 5 dsp sugar in milk and condensed milk over low heat, stirring all the time.
4. After the sugar has dissolved, add melted China grass and remove from heat.
5. Strain into a flat glass dish.
6. Arrange coconut scrapings over the pudding and refrigerate.
7. Roast grated coconut and 1 dsp sugar over low flame. Sprinkle over the pudding before serving.

*To serve 6*

# Breakfast Delights

1    Paalappam (Hoppers)

2    Idiappam (String Hoppers)

3    Puttu

4    Pathiri

5    Uppumav

6    Parotta

# Paalappam

**You will need :**

1. 2 1/2 dsp sugar
2. 1 tsp yeast
3. 2 cups water
4. 1/2 cup semolina
5. 1/4 kg rice flour, roasted and passed through a fine sieve
6. 2 cups coconut milk
7. salt to taste
8. appam vessel
9. gingelly oil

*To make 15*

**Method :**

1. Dissolve 1 tsp sugar and yeast in 1/2 cup warm water and keep aside for 20 minutes to let it rise.

2. Mix 1/2 cup semolina with 1 1/2 cups water and cook, then cool the gruel. Add to the rice flour. Knead well to make a soft dough. Add the fermented yeast mixture and knead again. Keep the dough covered. Set aside for 12 hours for the dough to rise. When the dough has risen well, add the coconut milk, the remaining sugar and salt to taste and make lace appams.

*To make the appams :*

Smear the appam vessel lightly with gingelly oil. Warm till moderately hot. Pour a ladleful of the batter into the vessel. Lift off the flame and swirl rapidly, once. Return to fire and cook with lid on for 1-2 min. Repeat till batter is used up.

*Note :*

Too much sugar will cause the appams to stick to the vessel.

# Idiappam
## (String Hoppers)

*You will need :*

1   1½ cups water
2   1 dsp refined vegetable oil
3   salt to taste
4   3 cups rice flour, roasted
5   1 cup coconut, grated
6   idli moulds

*Method :*

1   Bring water to boil. Add oil and salt. Remove from fire.
2   Pour the boiling water slowly into the rice flour, stirring all the time to prevent lumps.
3   Knead well to form a soft dough.
4   Divide the dough into small portions and press each portion through a semolina press onto a perforated plate.
5   Steam in idli moulds for 7 to 10 minutes.
6   Garnish with grated coconut. Serve hot with sweetened coconut milk, or any meat or vegetable stew.

*To make 20*

## Puttu

*You will need :*

1. salt to taste
2.  2 cups rice flour, slightly coarse
3. water as required
4. 1 cup coconut, grated
5. puttu maker

*Method :*

1. Add salt to flour. Sprinkle some water over the flour and mix lightly to form a dry mixture. Make sure lumps do not form.

2. Now fill up the tube of the puttu maker with coconut gratings, followed by rice flour. Do this alternately. Make sure you end with grated coconut. Fix the tube to the mouth of the pot from which the steam is rising. Close the free end of the tube with its perforated cap. Now raise the flame, so that the force of the steam increases to penetrate the flour and grated coconut. It is released at the top through the perforated cap. When the steam comes out forcefully, it means the puttu is done. Remove the tube from the pot and push the puttu out of the tube on to a plate with a rod.

3. Repeat the process with the rest of the rice flour. Serve hot.

*To serve 3*

Pathiri

### You will need :

1   1½ cups water
2   ½ tsp refined vegetable oil
3   salt to taste
4   1 cup fine rice flour
5   ½ cup thick coconut milk

*To make 10*

### Method :

1   Bring water to boil. Add oil and salt.
2   Lower the flame and add the flour, stirring well to prevent lumps. Cook over low heat till all the water is absorbed.
3   Remove from fire and knead well, without adding water, to make a soft dough.
4   Divide the dough into small balls, sprinkle with rice flour and roll out into thin round shapes. Trim the edges with a round cutter.
5   Place, one after the other, on a heated griddle (tava). Turn over after a few seconds and cook till it puffs up.
6   Remove from fire and smear with coconut milk.

### Note :

Best with mutton or chicken stew.

## Uppumav

*You will need :*

1 ½ cup refined vegetable oil
2 ½ tsp mustard seeds
3 2 tsp husked black beans
4 ½ cup onion, finely chopped
5 1 dsp green chillies, finely chopped
6 ½ dsp ginger, finely chopped
7 1 dsp curry leaves, chopped
8 2 cups semolina
9 6 cups water
10 1-2 dsp lime juice
11 ½ tsp salt
12 2 dsp broken cashewnuts, fried
13 a few coriander leaves

*To serve 6*

*Method :*

1 Heat the oil and splutter mustard seeds and beans. Add and sauté the onions, green chilles, ginger and curry leaves.
2 Add the semolina and mix well.
3 Add 6 cups boiling water to this mixture with lime juice, salt and cashewnuts.
4 Bring to boil. Stir continuously, allowing the water to be absorbed.
5 Remove from heat. Serve warm, garnished with coriander leaves.

## Parotta

*You will need :*

1   ¹/₂ kg refined flour
2   1 egg
3   1 tsp sugar
4   1 dsp curd ( not too sour )
5   milk as required
6   salt to taste
7   vegetable fat or ghee

*To serve 7*

*Method :*

1   Mix together ingredients 1 to 6 and make a loose dough. Pound and knead the dough for several minutes till it becomes soft and smooth. Cover with a wet cloth and leave the dough aside for 4 hours.

2   Knead again before making the parotta. Break a portion of the dough and shape it into a lime-sized ball. Roll it out, round and thin, on a floured stone or board. After rolling, spread warm ghee or fat on it. Now pleat lengthwise from one end to the other and twist into a round.

3   Flatten it again with the palm and fingers of your hand or roll it softly without applying pressure. Then cook on a hot, greased iron pan till both sides are well done.

4   Pile three or four parottas together and compress between your palms. This will separate the layers.

*Note :*

You can use water instead of milk, but the latter makes softer parottas.

# Teatime Favourites

1 Avalos Unda

2 Aval Vilayichathu (Puffed Rice in Jaggery)

3 Groundnut Chikki

4 Achappam (Flower-shaped Cookies)

5 Kuzhalappam

6 Ethekka Appam (Banana Fritters)

7 Parippu Vada (Lentil Cakes)

8 Vattayappam

9 Jackfruit Elayappam

10 Murukku

11 Unniappam

12 Black Halva

13 White Halva

14 Sharkara Puratti (Candied Banana Chips)

*Avalos Unda*

**You will need :**

1  1 cup sugar
2  $1/2$ cup water
3  1 dsp lime juice
4  1 dsp melted ghee
5  $1/4$ tsp cardamom powder
6  $1/2$ kg avalos powder (see below)

**For avalos powder :**

1  1 kg rice
2  6 cups coconut, grated
3  $1/2$ tsp cumin seeds
4  salt to taste

**Method :**

1  Mix sugar, water and lime juice. Keep on fire and cook to one-thread consistency. Add ghee, remove from fire, and sprinkle cardamom powder over.

2  Cool slightly and add the warm syrup to the avalos powder.

3  Mix well and shape into small balls, the size of limes.

4  Toss the balls lightly in avalos powder and store in an airtight tin.

**To make the avalos powder :**

1  Soak 1 kg rice in water. Drain and powder the slightly damp rice.
2  Sieve the flour and mix grated coconut into it with your fingers.
3  Add $1/2$ tsp cumin seeds and salt to taste. Mix well.
4  Compact the mixture in the bowl to retain the moisture, and set aside for 3 hours.
5  Lightly roast on a heavy skillet over medium heat, stirring constantly, till golden brown.
6  Remove from fire, cool and sieve to remove any lumps.
7  Powder the lumps and roast again and add to the prepared avalos powder.
8  Cool and store in airtight containers. Use as required.

*To make 20*

## Aval Vilayichathu
### (Puffed Rice in Jaggery)

*You will need :*

1   ¹/₄ cup melted ghee
2   ¹/₂ cup coconut slivers
3   ¹/₂ cup sesame seeds
4   1 cup roasted gram
5   1¹/₂ kg jaggery
6   3 cups water
7   4 coconuts, finely grated
8   ¹/₂ kg beaten rice
9   2 tsp cardamom powder

*Method :*

1   Heat ghee in a pan. Lightly fry coconut slivers, sesame seeds and roasted gram. Set aside.
2   Dissolve jaggery in 3 cups water. Heat over low flame to make 6 cups syrup. Strain.
3   Bring this syrup to boil in a heavy vessel. Add grated coconut and cook over a low flame, stirring constantly till one-thread consistency is reached.
4   Remove from fire. Cool slightly and add the beaten rice. Mix well. Add the fried ingredients along with cardamom powder.
5   Mix and cool. Store in a dry container.

*To serve 10*

*Groundnut Chikki*

*You will need :*

1    1 cup groundnuts, roasted
2    $^1/_2$ cup sugar
3    $^1/_4$ tsp butter
4    $^1/_4$ tsp bicarbonate of soda

*Method :*

1    Crumble groundnuts into small pieces.
2    Brown sugar in a heavy skillet and add butter.
3    Add bicarbonate of soda. When the mixture begins to froth, add the crumbled groundnuts. Remove from fire and mix well.
4    Pour into a greased tray or onto a marble slab and level the surface with a rolling pin.
5    Cut into desired shapes before the mixture hardens. Store in airtight containers.

*Note :*

Prolonged exposure to air will turn the chikki soggy.

*To make 12 pieces*

## Achappam
### (Flower-shaped Cookies)

*You will need :*

1   ¹/₂ kg fine rice flour
2   2 cups coconut milk
3   2 eggs, whisked
4   2 tsp sugar
5   2 tsp sesame seeds
6   1 tsp cumin seeds
7   salt to taste
8   coconut oil or refined vegetable oil for deep frying
9   achappam mould

*Method :*

1   Add coconut milk into the flour in small quantities, kneading all the time, to make a soft dough.
2   Gradually add the eggs and whisk to make a thick batter.
3   Stir in sugar, sesame seeds, cumin seeds and salt.
4   Heat oil in a wok and warm the achappam mould in it.
5   Take some batter in a small vessel and dip the hot mould into it, taking care not to immerse the mould completely.
6   Dip the mould coated with batter rapidly in the hot oil.
7   The achappam will float free in the oil. Turn over and fry till golden brown on both sides. Drain off excess oil and transfer to a paper. Store in airtight container.

*Note :*

Too much sugar in the batter will cause the achappam to stick to the mould.

*To make 30*

## Kuzhalappam

*You will need :*

1   2 cups coconut, finely grated
2   ¹/₂ kg fine rice flour
3   ¹/₂ tsp cumin seeds
4   ¹/₄ cup button onions
5   1 dsp garlic cloves
6   salt to taste
7   1 dsp sesame seeds
8   coconut oil or refined vegetable oil for frying

*Note :*

1   The dough should be well kneaded for crisp kuzhalappams.
2   When rolling out the dough, make only as many curls as can be fried at a time.

*To make 40*

*Method :*

1   Mix half the grated coconut into the rice flour lightly with the fingers to make a mixture free of lumps. Set aside.
2   Extract ¹/₂ cup milk from the remaining coconut.
3   Grind cumin seeds, button onions and garlic cloves to a fine paste. Dissolve the ground paste and salt in coconut milk.
4   Roast the coconut and rice flour mixture over a low flame in a heavy vessel, till fairly dry. Sprinkle the coconut milk over and continue stirring, till steam rises from the flour.
5   Remove from fire and knead well, adding enough water to form a soft dough.
6   Knead the sesame seeds into the dough, cover with a damp cloth and set aside for half an hour.
7   Divide the dough into small portions the size of large marbles.
8   Roll the dough into thin circles, on wax paper or greased banana leaves.
9   Wrap the rolled out dough around a greased rod and press the overlapping edges together to form a small curl. Slide it off the rod. Repeat till all the dough is used up.
10   Deep fry, cool and store in airtight containers.

# Ethekka Appam
## (Banana Fritters)

*You will need :*

1   6 ripe bananas, peeled
2   $1/2$ cup water
3   1 cup refined flour
4   $1/2$ cup rice flour
5   1 tsp sugar
6   a pinch of bicarbonate of soda
7   refined vegetable oil

*Method :*

1   Cut each banana into 3 pieces, lengthwise.
2   Make a thick batter with both the flours and $1/2$ cup water. Add sugar and bicarbonate of soda.
3   Dip the banana slices in the batter and deep fry in hot oil till golden brown.
4   Drain off the excess oil and serve hot.

*To serve 12*

# Parippu Vada
## (Lentil Cakes)

*You will need :*

1    1 cup pigeon peas
2    1/2 cup onion, finely chopped
3    1 dsp green chillies, chopped
4    1 tsp ginger, finely chopped
5    1 dsp curry leaves, finely chopped
6    1/2 tsp asafoetida powder
7    salt to taste
8    coconut oil or refined vegetable oil
     for deep frying

*Method :*

1    Soak the pigeon peas in water for one
     hour. Drain and grind to a coarse
     paste.
2    Add the remaining ingredients and
     mix well.
3    Shape into rounds, each the size of a
     large lime.
4    Flatten slightly, and deep fry in hot oil
     till golden brown.
5    Drain and serve hot.

*To serve 6*

Vatteappam

*You will need :*

1   8 1/4 dsp sugar
2   1/2 cup warm water
3   1/2 tsp yeast
4   1/2 cup semolina
5   1 1/2 cups water
6   1/4 kg fine rice flour
7   1 cup coconut, grated and ground to a paste
8   3/4 cup coconut milk
9   salt to taste
10  a few raisins

*Method :*

1   Dissolve 1 tsp sugar in warm water and sprinkle yeast in it. Allow it to froth.
2   Cook semolina with water to make a gruel. Allow it to cool.
3   Combine the flour, yeast and gruel to make a dough. Set aside to rise for 6 hours.
4   Add the ground coconut paste and dilute the dough with the coconut milk. Add salt and allow it to rise for six hours.
5   Pour into a 8" diametre greased mould. Place some raisins on top and steam in a pressure cooker without placing the weight. Cook for fifteen minutes. Cut into wedges and serve

*To serve 6*

## Jackfruit Elayappam

### To make Jackfruit preserve :

1   4 kg ripe jackfruit, mashed in a mixer
2   1 kg jaggery
3   4 cups water
4   20 gms ghee
5   1 tsp cardamom powder

### Method :

1   Dissolve jaggery in water. Strain into a heavy-bottomed vessel and cook over a low flame to make into a thick syrup. Add the mashed jackfruit into the jaggery syrup. Stir well. As it thickens, keep adding ghee, a little at a time. Mix well, remove from fire and add cardamom powder.

To serve 10

### For Elayappam :

1   2 cups jackfruit preserve
2   2 1/4 cups water
3   2 tsp refined vegetable oil
4   salt to taste
5   2 cups fine rice flour
6   1/4 cup sugar
8   1 cup coconut, grated
9   banana leaves
    cut into 10 cm x 10 cm sections

### Method :

1   Boil 2 cups water with oil and salt. Lower the flame and gradually stir in the flour.
2   Remove from fire, and knead well into a dough without any lumps. Divide the dough into eight portions.
3   Dissolve sugar in 1/4 cup water. Add grated coconut and cook over a low flame till the water is absorbed.
4   Remove from fire and add the jackfruit preserve. Mix well. Divide the mixture into 8 portions.
5   Clean and wipe dry banana leaves.
6   Spread a portion of the dough evenly on a leaf, with fingers. It should be spread thin.
7   Spread a portion of the jackfruit preserve evenly over one half of the dough. Fold over the other half. Press and seal the sides. Repeat till the dough and filling are used up.
8   Steam the elayappams for 30 minutes.

*Murukku*

You will need :

1   2 cups roasted gram
2   1 cup husked black beans
3   4 cups fine rice flour
4   10 cups water
5   salt to taste
6   1 dsp butter
7   1 dsp sesame seeds
8   1 dsp cumin seeds
9   groundnut oil or refined vegetable oil
    for frying

*Method :*

1   Powder the roasted gram and black beans separately.
2   Sieve the rice flour and the powdered ingredients together.
3   Boil water and add salt and butter to it.
4   Add boiled water slowly into the sieved flours, stirring all the time to prevent lumps.
5   Cool and knead into a soft dough, adding the sesame and cumin seeds.

*To make the murukku :*

1   Divide the dough into several small portions.
2   Place a portion of the dough in a murukku press. Press the dough through onto a lightly floured surface, to form spiralling rounds. Deep fry in batches in hot oil, till done. Drain off excess oil, cool and store in airtight tins.

*To make 50*

# Unniappam

*You will need :*

1. 100 gms jaggery, grated
2. 1 cup water
3. 1 cup fine rice flour
4. ¹/₂ cup coconut, finely chopped and fried in ghee
5. ¹/₂ cup mashed ripe bananas
6. 1 dsp sugar
7. ¹/₈ tsp bicarbonate of soda

*Method :*

1. Melt jaggery in 1 cup water and cook to make a thick syrup.
2. Mix all the ingredients together thoroughly in a bowl to form a soft, thick batter of dropping consistency.
3. Drop spoonfuls of the batter into hot oil and deep fry till golden brown. If an unniappam pan is available, fry batter in hot oil, turning over till both sides are golden brown.

*To serve 10*

## Black Halva

### You will need :

1. 6 litres water
2. ¹/₂ kg refined flour
3. 1³/₄ kg jaggery
4. 12 cups coconut milk, extracted from 3 medium-size coconuts
5. 250 gms ghee
6. ¹/₂ cup sugar
7. ¹/₂ tsp cardamom powder
8. 100 gms cashewnut slivers

### Note :

While making halva, use a high steady flame at first, gradually reducing the heat as the cooking progresses.

The halva should be cooked slowly over 2 to 2¹/₂ hours.

### Method :

1. Using 2 cups water, knead the flour well to make a soft dough.
2. Reserve 3 cups water and add the rest a little at a time to the dough to make thin batter.
3. Strain the batter through a muslin cloth to remove any lumps.
4. Set aside for a few hours and decant the clean liquid from the top.
5. Melt the jaggery in 6 cups water and strain.
6. Mix the batter, jaggery syrup and coconut milk together in a heavy vessel. The consistency should be that of milk.
8. Bring to boil, stirring constantly, till quite thick. Stir in the ghee in small quantities, stirring all the time, till the mixture forms a soft ball.
9. Add sugar, cardamom powder and half the cashewnut slivers.
10. Cook over low heat till the ghee separates.
11. Remove from fire and pour into a greased tray. Sprinkle the remaining cashewnut slivers on top and smooth the surface.

*To make 50 pieces*

# White Halva

**You will need :**

1   6 litres water
2   ¹/₂ kg refined flour
3   1¹/₂ kg sugar
4   2 litres milk
5   250 gms ghee
6   ¹/₂ cup sugar
7   ¹/₂ tsp cardamom powder
8   100 gms cashewnut slivers

*Note :*

While making the halva, use a strong flame at first, gradually lowering the heat as the cooking progresses.

**Method :**

1   Using 2 cups water, knead the flour well to make a soft dough.
2   Reserve 3 cups water and add the rest a little at a time to the dough to make thin batter.
3   Strain the batter through a muslin cloth to remove any lumps.
4   Set aside for a few hours and decant clean liquid from the top.
5   Dissolve 1¹/₂ kg sugar in 3 cups water. Strain and set aside.
6   Mix the batter, sugar syrup and milk together in a heavy vessel. Bring to boil, stirring continuously.
7   As it thickens, add the ghee, stirring all the time.
8   Cook over a low flame till the oil separates.
9   Add ¹/₂ cup sugar, cardamom powder and half of the cashewnuts slivers. Stir well.
10  Transfer to a greased plate and spread evenly. Place the remaining cashewnuts slivers on top.

*To make 50 pieces*

# Sharkara Puratti
## (Candied Banana Chips)

*You will need :*

1  ½ kg plantains, not too
   mature
2  refined vegetable oil
   for frying
3  ¼ kg jaggery
4  ½ tsp cumin powder
5  ½ tsp dried ginger
   powder
6  2 tsp rice flour
7  1 tsp sugar

*To serve 10*

*Method :*

1  Pare the bananas, wash and dry well.
2  Slice into thin, round sections of even thickness.
3  Deep fry the slices in hot oil till crisp.
4  Sprinkle a little salt water in the oil. Stir again so
   that the salt is evenly absorbed by the chips.
   When the spluttering subsides, remove the
   chips from the oil, place in a strainer and let
   the oil drain away.
5  Dissolve the jaggery in water. Strain and heat
   to make a syrup of one-thread consistency.
6  Lower the flame and stir the banana chips into
   the syrup. Mix well to coat the chips uniformly
   with the syrup.
7  Sprinkle the cumin and dried ginger powders.
   Stir well, taking care not to break the chips.
8  Remove from fire and sprinkle over with a
   mixture of rice flour and sugar. Stir till separated
   and dry. Cool and store in airtight containers.

*Note :*

Use only mature but unripe bananas to make
the chips.

# Notes for the Kitchen

A 225 ml cup has been used as the basic measure in this book. Also used are teaspoon (tsp)—equivalent to 5 ml—and dessertspoon (dsp)—equivalent to 10 ml—measures. The adjacent picture is indicative of the relative spoon measures.

Coffee Spoon
Teaspoon
Dessertspoon

For convenience, here is a list of some of the lentils and other ingredients used, with their equivalents in Malayalam and Hindi :

| Bengal Gram | : Kadala Parippu | : Chana Dal |
|---|---|---|
| Black-eyed Beans | : Van Payaru | : Lobiya |
| Gram Flour | : Besan | |
| Husked Black Beans | : Uzhunnu Parippu | : Urad Dal |
| Husked Green Beans | : Cherupayar Parippu | : Moong Dal |
| Pigeon Peas | : Tovara Parippu | : Arhar/Toor Dal |
| Refined Flour | : Maida | |
| Whole Bengal Gram | : Kadala | : Kala Chana |
| Whole Green Beans | : Cheru Payaru | : Sabut Moong |

Urali

Vermicelli press

Puttu maker

Appam chatti

Meen chatti

# Spices and Condiments

**Asafoetida** is available both as powder and granules. It is also sold as a hard lump that can be crushed or ground for use. Asafoetida has a strong aroma, so very little is sufficient to flavour a dish. In Kerala, it is used in combination with fenugreek seeds in sambar and pickles.

**Button onions** are a type of small purple onion with a strong flavour. In Kerala, it is used as an ingredient and for seasoning.

**Cocum** is a fruit grown in the western coast of India. The orange-sized fruit has deep purple flesh surrounding a large seed. It is picked when ripe and the thick lobes of the fruit are cut and dried on mats in the sun. The rind is almost black in colour and imparts a pale purplish hue when soaked in water. Popular in Syrian Christian cuisine, cocum—also called fish tamarind (kodampuli)—is used in several fish preparations. It is first soaked in water and then added to curry to give a distinctive sour taste. It also acts as a preservative in fish curries.

**Coconut** is used extensively in the cuisines of Kerala. The fleshy part of it is grated and used either separately or ground with spices to make the masala base for several preparations.

**Coconut Milk** is also used in several kinds of curries and desserts. The milk is extracted in two stages:

Put 2 cups grated coconut in a blender and liquidize with $2 \frac{1}{2}$ cups hot water. Strain, squeezing out as much liquid as possible. This will yield about $1 \frac{1}{2}$ cups thick coconut milk. Repeat this process using the same coconut gratings and another $2 \frac{1}{2}$ cups hot water. This will give 2 cups 'thin milk'. The first milk is richer in content and will curdle if boiled, so it is added at the end of the cooking. The second milk is watery and can be cooked for a long time.

**Curry leaves** are ground with coconut and other ingredients to make a chutney. They are also used as seasoning with mustard seeds and dry red chillies.

**Ghee**, or clarified butter, is derived by melting unsalted butter and cooking on low heat for about 50 minutes and straining through a cheese cloth to remove the brown solids. It can be bottled and preserved without refrigeration.

Asafoetida

Button Onions

Cocum

Coconut

Grated Coconut

Curry Leaves

Cinnamon

Clove

Cardamom